Remembrance

Remembrance

The Dhikr
of the Inayati Sufis

Edited from Talks by
Pir Netanel Miles-Yépez

Albion
Andalus
Boulder, Colorado
2016

"The old shall be renewed,
and the new shall be made holy."
— Rabbi Avraham Yitzhak Kook

Albion-Andalus, Inc.
P. O. Box 19852
Boulder, CO 80308
www.albionandalus.com

Cover design by Daryl McCool
Design and layout by Albion-Andalus Books
"Rose-Heart and Wings" illustration
© 2008 Netanel Miles-Yépez

Manufactured in the United States of America

ISBN-13: 978-0692738337 (Albion-Andalus Books)
ISBN-10: 0692738339

CONTENTS

ACKNOWLEDGEMENTS

THIS LITTLE BOOK is based upon three talks given to the Inayati Sufi Study and Practice group at Naropa University in Boulder, Colorado, in the Fall of 2014. I wish to thank: Giovannina Jobson, the Contemplative Affairs Coordinator at Naropa who arranged for the practice space for us each semester; my friend, Pouria Montazeri, who helped start the first sessions off on the right foot; Daniel Battigalli-Ansell, who was the heart of the group and held the space beautifully week after week; Peggy Anderson, Jason Cabitac, Brad Carhill, Mary Chavers, Chuck Davis, Allison DeHart, Jenna Jennings, Rhea Nicole Johnson, Samantha Krezinski, Jay Mannan Maitri, Marie Mannat, Stephanie Miller, Carla Burns Mueller, Chloe Pappas, James Peacock, Robbie Tesar, Raj Seymour, Arthur Van Siclen, Jemila Spain, Cynthia St. Clair, Yasha Wagner, and the many others who attended these sessions through the Spring of 2016.

I am likewise grateful to those others for whom I refined this presentation, and who contributed to my own understanding of *dhikr* as I led it on various occasions over the last several years, including: the students in my Contemplative Islam and Religion and Mystical Experience courses at Naropa University; my independent study students in Sufism, Lucas Sego and Daji Tudeng; my friends and colleagues, Stephanie Yuhas and Zvi Ish-Shalom, in whose courses I also taught *dhikr* and Sufism; Jennifer Alia Wittman who invited me to teach and lead *dhikr* at the Abode of the Message in New Lebanon, New York, in the summer of 2015; and Darakshan Farber who invited me to lead *dhikr* at Meditation Mount in Ojai, California in the Fall of 2015.

— Netanel Mu'in ad-Din al-Maimuni
  Boulder, Colorado
  June 10th, 2016

Remembrance

The Dhikr
of the Inayati Sufis

SESSION ONE
DISCOVERING THE DIVINITY WITHIN

IN SUFISM, we sit together in a circle to emphasize our unity. The Sufi circle is called a *ḥalqah,* or 'ring,' the symbol of our commitment to one another. In this 'ring,' we are bound as in a marriage to the sharing of an experience. Thus, a small group or community of Sufis is also usually called a *ḥalqah* or 'circle,' because of what is shared between them.

The *ḥalqah* formed for spiritual practice describes the boundaries of a ritual space. For this reason, we form and enter it intentionally, with an invocation. The invocation of the Inayati Sufis was taught to us by Pir-o-Murshid Hazrat Inayat Khan and may be performed in the following way:

1. Hold out your hands, palms up.
2. Place your right palm in the center of your chest.
3. Place your left palm on top of your right hand.
4. Place the thumb of your right hand over that of your left hand.
5. Spread your fingers wide like the wings of an

eagle.

6. Lift your gaze heavenward.

7. Now let your chin descend to your chest, as you say, "This is not my body."

8. Turn your chin to your left shoulder.

9. Now allow your head to loll and drift across your chest to your right shoulder, as you say, "This is the temple of the heart."[1]

We then call "Toward the One" and recite a prayer of the same name by Hazrat Inayat Khan, the primary prayer of the Inayati Sufis:

Toward the One,
The Perfection of Love, Harmony, and Beauty,
The Only Being,
United with all the Illuminated Souls
Who form the embodiment of the Master,
The Spirit of Guidance.

In this way, we create and enter a ritual space and atmosphere. The primary ritual or spiritual practice done in this atmosphere is called *dhikr* (the *dh* is pronounced with a soft *th* sound). The word, *dhikr* or *zekr* means 'remembrance.' (These are merely the Arabic and Farsi pronunciations of the same word.) Which is to say, *dhikr* is a practice of 'remembering' divinity and the divine unity, of being in continual 'remembrance' of the holy ground of our being through repetition of a divine name, a sacred formula or phrase.

The most celebrated and important sacred phrase for Sufis is *Lā 'ilāha 'illā llāh.* You might recognize this as the first part of the great creedal statement of Islam, the *shahāda* or *kalimah.* Literally, it means, 'There is no god but God,' which is to say, 'There are no other gods beside *Allāh.'*

In the Arabian Peninsula, in the time of the Prophet Muhammad, peace and blessings be upon him, this was a radical statement of monotheism in an otherwise polytheistic tribal culture, advancing the understanding of divinity in that time. It was a unifying idea. Instead of being divided among a host of local deities, the Arabian tribes united under one God, saying, 'There is no god but God.'

But, as you might have guessed, Sufis read a still deeper meaning in this phrase, often breaking the phrase into two distinct parts, *Lā 'ilāha* and *'illā llāh,* changing the emphasis of the entire statement.

Lā 'ilāha means exactly what it says, 'There is no God.' No matter where you look, whether under a microscope or through a telescope, you won't find God. Which is to say, in the objective universe, in the material universe of science, you will not find God. This is our experience of the material world. And the Sufi acknowledges this fact, this aspect of our universe, with the declaration, *Lā 'ilāha,* 'There is no God.'

But that's not where it ends for the Sufi. For the second part of the statement says, *'illā llāh,* 'nevertheless, God.' Here, in my heart, I have a sense of something sacred, whether I call it divinity or not. For one person, it may be a simple longing for something *Other,* something

Greater; and for another, it may be an actual experience of holiness, of the sacred, that cannot be proven, but which, at the same time, cannot be un-experienced.

You see, while we must concede that, in the world of the senses, there is no observable or demonstrable God, nevertheless, there is sometimes within us, an inner *shahāda* or 'testimony' that is continually whispering to us, "God." This is why the philosopher Martin Buber liked to describe faith as "holy insecurity."[2] For while I may not be able to prove it to you, I cannot deny it to myself. It is an insecure faith, a sense of something holy I cannot anchor in certainty. Faith is the inner testimony of things unseen. And this is what the statement, *Lā 'ilāha 'illā llāh,* describes . . . a paradox of objective and subjective experience, the marriage and mingling of two realities.

On another level, however, *Lā 'ilāha 'illā llāh,* 'There is no god but God,' is also interpreted by Sufis to mean, 'Nothing exists except divinity.' It is an acknowledgement of a unified or unifying wholeness, the sacred substratum of all existence. But perhaps this is another discussion for another time, as that is not necessarily something to be merely accepted, but something to discover through experience.

To this basic statement, the simple phrase, *Lā 'ilāha 'illā llāh,* the Sufi often adds the word, *hū,* which literally means 'he' in Arabic; though among Sufis, it is, paradoxically, code for the divine feminine, which is to say, for the experiential presence of God, the sacred known and felt through experience.

THE CHISHTI-INAYATI DHIKR

Now every Sufi lineage has its own way of approaching *dhikr,* using the sacred phrase, *Lā 'ilāha 'illā llāh hū,* with different melodies, different body movements, and even different pronunciations. In the Inayati lineage of Hazrat Inayat Khan, which is derived from the older Chishti lineage of Central Asia and India, *Lā 'ilāha 'illā llāh hū* is broken into four parts and performed in the following way:

Lā 'ilāha—'There is no god.'

Begin by pointing your chin at your left shoulder. Then, allow your head to loll, drifting down, carried by its own weight and momentum across your chest toward your right shoulder, continuing to arc upward until your face is exposed to the heavens. As your head makes this 270-degree arc, pronounce the words, *Lā 'ilāha,* accompanied by the thought, 'There is no God.' This is a movement of expansion, of evolution, looking out into the material universe and finding only space ... not God.

'Illā—'nevertheless.'

Now allow your head to fall forward, and your chin to drop straight onto your chest, as you say, *'illā,* 'nevertheless.' In doing this, we descend inward, looking for our own experience, no longer dependent on our external senses and what we are told in the external world. It is here where we begin to discover something for ourselves.

Llāh—'God.'

Lift your chin off your chest and gently throw your head back, so that you are again facing the heavens. While making this movement, you say, *llāh*, 'God!' In the exultation of discovery within, we lift our heads in celebration of what has been discovered—God in our highest ideal!

Hū—'the one who is.'

Now allow your head to drift slowly and gently down and to the left, settling over you heart, as if magnetically drawn there, as you pronounce, *hū*. We settle consciousness back in the heart, where we actually experience God through the resonant *hū*, the vibration awakening the heart, knocking on the door of the heart, which opens on divinity itself.

Having investigated the world in a wide arc, a spiral, in a fruitless search for God outside ourselves, we finally turn inward. There, finding something personal, something true to us, an ideal, we ascend the same pole at the center of our being (which we have just descended), lifting our heads high, buoyed by the exultation of self-discovery. And yet, this is not actually an experience of divinity. It is only an ideal. The experience of divinity is only found in our hearts.

Vocal Dhikr

The Inayati *dhikr* can be practiced silently or out loud. Out loud it is called *dhikr jahri.* We do this pronouncing the vowels in the four parts of *Lā 'ilāha 'illā llāh* with aspiration (the exhalation of breath) and a soft lion-like growl, accompanying the words with deep intention. To keep count, we use a string of ninety-nine beads called a *tasbīḥ,* a 'tool of glorification.'

Now let's do a round together.

Lā 'ilāha 'illā llāh hū (99x slowly)

Did you notice how the *dhikr* tends to go on, even after it stops? *Dhikr* creates a flywheel in consciousness, so that, even when the words and the movements stop—often of their own accord—the remembrance goes on . . . *Lā 'ilāha 'illā llāh hū.* And that is the point or purpose of the practice, to take us from the act of *remembering* to actual *remembrance.*

To use our *tasbīḥ* and recite a *wazifa,* or mantra, is a purposeful activity that we direct, consciously. It is something that we are doing—*remembering.* But, at a certain point, we often find that we are no longer directing it consciously; it is as if something is being done to, or through us. The remembering is just happening now; it is apparently autonomous. That is being *in remembrance,* which is the goal of *dhikr,* to be in constant remembrance of God, or the sacred.[3]

We then close the ritual very much as we began it, with a dedication:

1. Hold out your hands, palms up.
2. Place your right palm in the center of your chest.
3. Place your left palm on top of your right hand.
4. Place the thumb of your right hand over that of your left hand.
5. Spread your fingers wide like the wings of an eagle.
6. Lift your gaze heavenward.
7. Now let your chin descend to your chest, as you say, "This is not my body."
8. Turn your chin to your left shoulder.
9. Now allow your head to loll and drift across your chest to your right shoulder, as you say, "This is the temple of God."

In the invocation, at the beginning of practice, the intention is to go inward. So we say, "This is the temple of the heart." But at the end, as we are about to re-enter the world, we affirm that this body is "The temple of God," dedicated to God and God's service.

Amin.

SESSION TWO
BUILDING A TEMPLE FOR THE
DIVINE PRESENCE

PIR VILAYAT INAYAT KHAN, the son of Hazrat Inayat Khan, used to talk about traditional Sufi practices as "building a temple for the Divine Presence." Likewise, he said that the Inayati form of *dhikr,* or 'remembrance' practice, is like "circumambulating the temple."[4]

This is a good way of looking at *dhikr* and other Sufi practices in general. These practices help us to make a sacred temple out of this body, sacralizing what we have allowed to become profane, or at least which we have forgotten is inherently holy. So, in some sense, our practices are done to re-claim and re-dedicate the body as a temple of the Divine Presence that dwells within it. The particular form of the Inayati *dhikr* then—with its spiraling movements—is like circumambulating that sacred 'temple' where God dwells in the heart.

Likewise, there is a way of looking at the *dhikr* as concentrating and spreading energy, building magnetism in the field around one's body. For the first movement of the *dhikr* is creating, as Pir Vilayat put it, a centrifugal force "expanding your consciousness into the galaxies," but also spreading energy, enriching the room in which you do your practice.[5]

This is important, because it is clear that spaces can acquire a definite presence. There are meditation halls I've known that are not simply empty rooms when you walk into them, but which are rich with a stillness and a quality of peacefulness that can be felt, almost palpably. And it is much easier to meditate in a such a place, because the atmosphere is already supporting and conducive to the process and state of meditation. It allows you to drop right into that particular mode.

So that is building magnetism in the field around us. But, in the second movement of *dhikr,* we are responding to the centripetal forces of our being and the "pull of the center," the solar plexus, "a gate in the center of the centrifuge," where, Pir Vilayat says, "the whole universe gets processed in your being like the water in a lake is processed in the vortex."[6] In the downward and upward movements of the *dhikr,* we are connecting to the axis, or pole center of our being, building magnetism near the heart-center.

SILENT DHIKR

Now, as I said before, Sufi *dhikr* can be practiced in two basic forms: *dhikr jahri* (vocal remembrance) and *dhikr khafi* (silent remembrance). Previously, we learned and practiced the Inayati *dhikr* in its audible form, *jahri,* performing the four movements of the *dhikr* and pronouncing the words of the *shahāda—Lā 'ilāha 'illā llāh hū,* which may be translated, 'There is no god; nevertheless, God Is.' But now we are going to do it in its silent or *khafi* form (also known as *dhikr-i-qalbi,* 'remembrance of the heart').

We'll perform the same four movements, but this time, we'll remember the words in our hearts alone, and accompany the movements with a specific four-part breathing pattern (inhaling and exhaling through the nostrils): 1. Exhalation; 2. Inhalation; 3. Inhalation; 4. Retention.

All together, the *dhikr khafi* practice goes like this:

Lā 'ilāha—'There is no god.'

Begin by pointing your chin at your left shoulder. Then, exhale fully through your nostrils as you allow your head to loll, drifting down and across your chest toward your right shoulder, continuing to arc upward until your face is exposed to the heavens. As your head makes this 270-degree arc, you mentally 'pronounce,' *Lā 'ilāha.*

'Illā—'nevertheless.'

Inhaling, allow your head to fall forward and your chin to drop straight onto your chest as you mentally pronounce, *'illā,* 'nevertheless.'

Llāh—'God.'

Inhaling deeper still, lift your chin off your chest and gently throw your head back, so that you are again facing the heavens. While making this movement, you mentally pronounce, *llāh,* 'God.'

Hū—'he,' or 'the one who is.'

Now, holding your breath as long as is comfortable for you, allow your head to drift gently down and to the left, settling over your heart, as you mentally pronounce, *hū.*

Follow me now in doing these four movements in silence, reciting the words inwardly with deep intention and following the aforementioned breathing pattern.

Lā 'ilāha 'illā llāh hū (11x slowly, silently)

You see, there are two 'temples' that are created and 'circumambulated' in this practice. One of your own body, and a greater one formed by all of us in practicing together—the Divine Presence dwelling in the space between us. Going around and around, we infuse the temple with the energy of the practice, charging and building the field of energy and saturating the space with sacred intention, re-dedicating the temple of the body and dedicating another greater temple formed by our communion with each other.

Now, if you are doing the practice using very deep inhalations and exhalations through the nostrils, it is enough to do it just three times (as Hazrat Inayat Khan suggests). Believe me, it's enough. Try it and you'll see.

It is perfect for restoring yourself quickly, returning and reorienting your awareness to the Beloved whenever necessary. But, in doing this practice, make sure that you hold the breath long enough in the retention phase to challenge your comfort zone a little. *Not too much.* You don't want to pass out or cause yourself to panic. That's not the purpose. Be sensible. Just make sure you aren't leaving the retention phase too quickly. If possible, stay with it long enough to feel your heartbeat in the silence of the held breath.

Amin.

SESSION THREE
FILLING-OUT THE
LAYERS OF REMEMBRANCE

AS I HAVE SAID, every Sufi lineage has its own way of approaching *dhikr*. Up to this point, we have been practicing *dhikr* in the way of the Chishti Sufis, as the universalist Inayati lineage is an off-shoot of the Chishti lineage. But Hazrat Inayat Khan actually made a unique contribution to the Chishti *dhikr* in his lifetime. Being one the greatest Indian classical musicians of his time, Inayat Khan composed a special melody for singing the *dhikr,* using the melodic mode known as Raag Bhairavi.

In this practice, we continue to use the four movements of the basic Chishti-Inayati *dhikr,* but layer onto the practice the special melody of Hazrat Inayat Khan, which is in turn broken into four parts.

But before we learn the melody and how to break it down, let's review the basic form of the *dhikr:*

Lā 'ilāha—'There is no god.'

Begin by pointing your chin at your left shoulder. Then, allow your head to loll, drifting down and across your chest toward your right shoulder, and continuing to arc upward until your face is exposed to the heavens. As your head makes this 270-degree arc, pronounce the words, *Lā 'ilāha.*

'Illā—'nevertheless.'

Allow your head to fall forward and your chin to drop straight onto your chest, as you say, *'illā,* 'nevertheless.'

Llāh—'God.'

Lift your chin off your chest and gently throw your head straight back, so that you are again facing the heavens. While making this movement, you say, *'llāh,* 'God.'

Hū—'he,' or 'the one who is.'

Now allow your head to drift gently down and to the left, settling over you heart, as you pronounce, *hū.*

So follow me now in these four movements, pronouncing the vowels with aspiration (the exhalation of breath) and a soft lion-like growl, accompanying the words with deep intention:

Lā 'ilāha 'illā llāh hū (11x slowly)

Now, let's add-in the melody of Hazrat Inayat Khan to the *dhikr:*

We'll do the melody slowly at first with the accompanying movements of the *dhikr* four times—two low, one high, and a final one, low.

So one part of the *dhikr* will be done like this. But slowly, through the *dhikr*, we'll break the phrase down into smaller and smaller parts.

19

The next part will be like this:

Then, it will break down further to:

And finally, simply:

Okay, so let's do a round of it together. Join in as soon as you catch hold of the melody:

> *Lā 'ilāha 'illā llāh hū* (99x slowly)
> *'illā llāh hū* (66x slowly)
> *āllāh hū* (33x slowly)
> *hū* (11x slowly)

This is a practice for creating *hadhrat,* or 'presence'—the same honorific given to *Hazrat* Inayat Khan—allowing us to feel it in our hearts and with each other. That presence is especially clear in the deep resonance created in the final vocalizations of *hū.*

LAYERS OF THE DHIKR

At this point, having added yet another layer to our practice of *dhikr,* it may seem that the practice has become very complicated, that it is impossible to maintain the proper awareness of every aspect of the *dhikr.* But this really isn't a problem, as every aspect of the *dhikr* is actually a prayer in itself. And I would suggest that you try to think about them as such, considering how they may work together to build the most complete experience.

Begin your *dhikr* by making your movements beautiful, for they are themselves a choreographed prayer to God, mimicking the elegant curves and bold strokes of Arabic calligraphy. The aesthetic dimension is important in Sufism as an element of spiritual practice, as it says in the *hadith,* "God is beautiful and loves beauty."[7] Just doing them mindfully, in an aesthetically pleasing way, is already a sign of your remembrance and a pure offering of the body to God.

Once you have established yourself in the movements of prayer, you can add the 'liturgy' to them—*Lā 'ilāha 'illā llāh hū.* And this is even better, because there are now good words of remembrance—with their own sacred vibration, connected to all the utterances of them through the centuries—upon your lips and entering the atmosphere. And these too, we can make beautiful, pronouncing them with love and attention to their sounds.

But it is not long before you discover that the words can easily be said while your mind and attention are wandering off, far into the distance. So, to a simple recitation of the words, we need to add the ingredient of awareness—attention to the words as we are pronouncing them, even holding tight to them, if need be.

When that is accomplished and comfortable, we find that we can also add another layer of conscious content to our attention—a layer of intentionality—a private message encoded in the carrier wave of the words. This might be as simple as a personally meaningful translation of the Arabic, accompanying the four movements and parts of the phrase in Arabic with a private translation: "There is no God; nevertheless, God's Presence." For instance, using "There is no God" with *Lā 'ilāha,* "nevertheless" with *'illā,* "God's" with *llāh,* and "Presence" with *hū.* This is as if to say, 'God's Presence is right here, in my heart.' It may not be a literal translation, but it is accurate to the intention.

So, again, every aspect of the *dhikr* is good in itself and an accomplishment of remembrance on its own, not to be discounted. But upon each we can also add a layer that increases the impact and significance of the *dhikr.*

APPENDIX
MUHAMMAD AL-GHAZZALI'S
CLASSIC DESCRIPTION OF DHIKR

LET YOUR HEART be in such a state that the existence or non-existence of anything is the same—that is, let there be no dichotomy of positive and negative. Then sit alone in a quiet place, free of any task or preoccupation, be it the reciting of the Qur'an, thinking about its meaning, concern over the dictates of religion, or what you have read in books—let nothing besides God enter the mind. Once you are seated in this manner, start to pronounce with your tongue, "Allah, Allah" keeping your thought on it.

Practice this continuously and without interruption; you will reach a point when the motion of the tongue will cease, and it will appear as if the word just flows from it spontaneously. You go on in this way until every trace of the tongue movement disappears while the heart registers the thought or the idea of the word.

As you continue with this invocation, there will come a time when the word will leave the heart completely. Only the palpable essence or reality of the name will remain, binding itself ineluctably to the heart.

Up to this point everything will have been dependent on your own conscious will; the divine bliss and enlightenment that may follow have nothing to do with your conscious will or choice. What you have done so far is to open the window, as it were. You have laid yourself exposed to what God may breathe upon you, as He has done upon his prophets and saints.

If you follow what is said above, you can be sure that the light of Truth will dawn upon your heart. At first intermittently, like flashes of lightning, it will come and go. Sometimes when it comes back it may stay longer than other times. Sometimes it may stay only briefly.[8]

NOTES

1. The placement of the hands, creating a symbolic eagle and winged heart, as well as this last phrase, "This is the temple of the heart," are particular adaptations of the Inayati-Maimuni lineage.

2. Martin Buber. *Israel and the World: Essays in a Time of Crisis.* New York: Schocken Books, 1948: 21-24.

3. See the Appendix and Muhammad al-Ghazzali's classic description of *dhikr*.

4. Vilayat Inayat Khan. *Awakening: A Sufi Experience.* New York: Jeremy P. Tarcher, 1999: 166, 176.

5. Vilayat Inayat Khan, "The Practice of Dhikr," *Chishtia Inayati Dhikr,* 2, a privately printed booklet of the Sufi Order International, ca. 2000.

6. Ibid., 2, 3.

7. *Sahih Muslim.*

8. Kabir Helminski. *The Knowing Heart: A Sufi Path of Transformation.* Boston: Shambhala Publications, 1999: 98-99.

Netanel Miles-Yépez

PIR NETANEL MU'IN AD-DIN MILES-YÉPEZ is the current head of the Inayati-Maimuni lineage of Sufism. He studied History of Religions at Michigan State University and Contemplative Religion at the Naropa Institute before pursuing traditional studies in both Sufism and Hasidism with Zalman Schachter-Shalomi and various other teachers. He has been deeply involved in ecumenical dialogue. He is the translator of *My Love Stands Behind a Wall: A Translation of the Song of Songs and Other Poems* (2015), the co-author of the critically acclaimed commentary on Hasidic spirituality, *A Heart Afire: Stories and Teachings of the Early Hasidic Masters* (2009), the editor of various works on InterSpirituality, including *Meditations for InterSpiritual Practice* (2012), and the editor of a new series of the works of the Sufi master, Hazrat Inayat Khan, annotated and adapted into modern English. He teaches "Contemplative Islam" and "Sufism" in the Department of Religious Studies at Naropa University.

Printed in Great Britain
by Amazon

32830706R00020